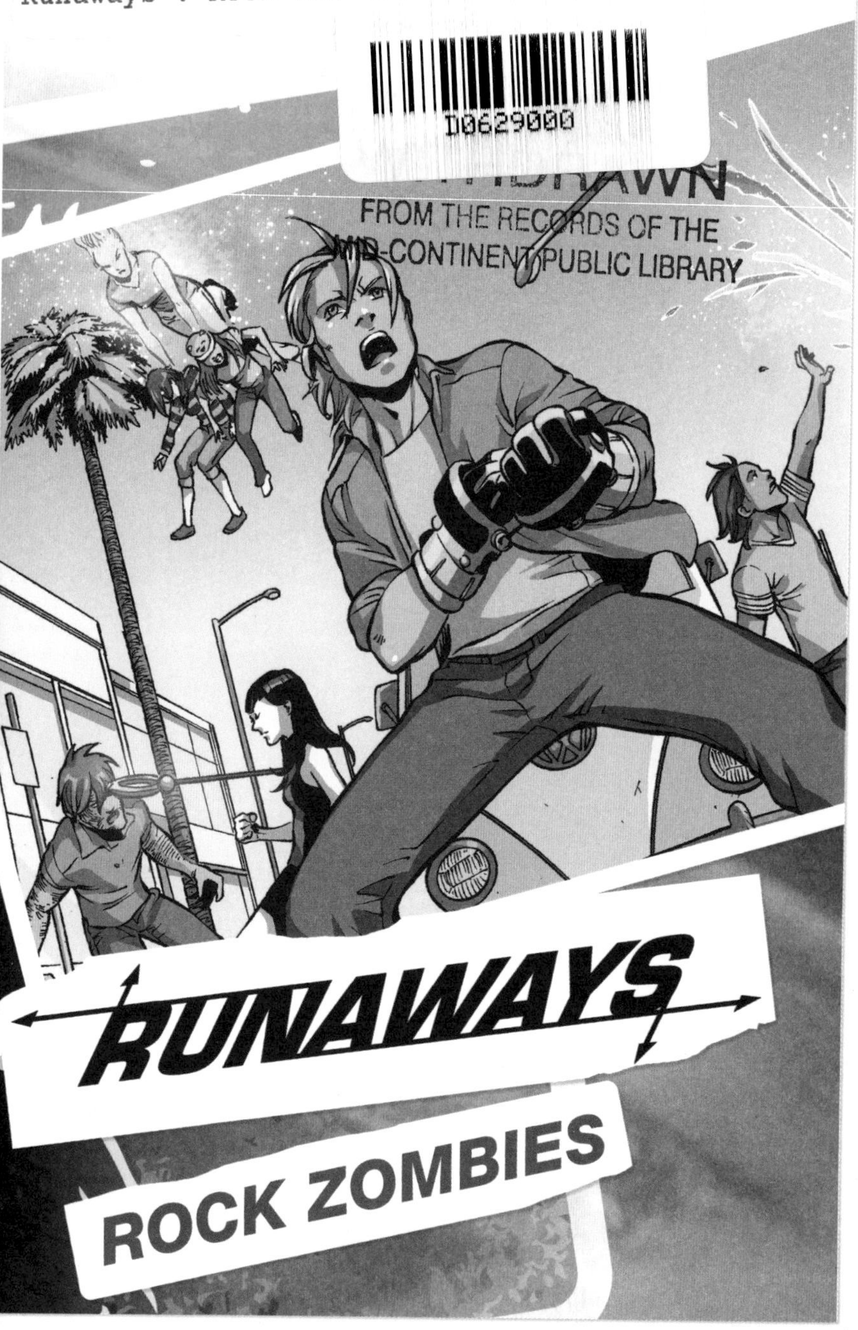

RUNAWAYS

ROCK ZOMBIES

RUNAWAYS

ROCK ZOMBIES

WRITER: **TERRY MOORE**
PENCILER: **TAKESHI MIYAZAWA**
INKERS: **TAKESHI MIYAZAWA, NORMAN LEE** &
CRAIG YEUNG
COVER ART: **HUMBERTO RAMOS** & **CHRISTINA STRAIN**

"MOLLIFEST DESTINY"
WRITER: **CHRIS YOST**
ARTIST: **SARA PICHELLI**

"TRUTH OR DARE"
WRITER: **JAMES ASMUS**
ARTIST: **EMMA RIOS**
COVER ART: **DAVID LAFUENTE** & **CHRISTINA STRAIN**

COLORIST: **CHRISTINA STRAIN**
LETTERER: **VC'S JOE CARAMAGNA**
EDITORS: **NICK LOWE** & **DANIEL KETCHUM**

RUNAWAYS CREATED BY **BRIAN K. VAUGHAN** & **ADRIAN ALPHONA**

COLLECTION EDITOR: **JENNIFER GRÜNWALD**
ASSISTANT EDITOR: **ALEX STARBUCK**
ASSOCIATE EDITOR: **JOHN DENNING**
EDITOR, SPECIAL PROJECTS: **MARK D. BEAZLEY**
SENIOR EDITOR, SPECIAL PROJECTS: **JEFF YOUNGQUIST**
SENIOR VICE PRESIDENT OF SALES: **DAVID GABRIEL**

EDITOR IN CHIEF: **JOE QUESADA**
PUBLISHER: **DAN BUCKLEY**
EXECUTIVE PRODUCER: **ALAN FINE**

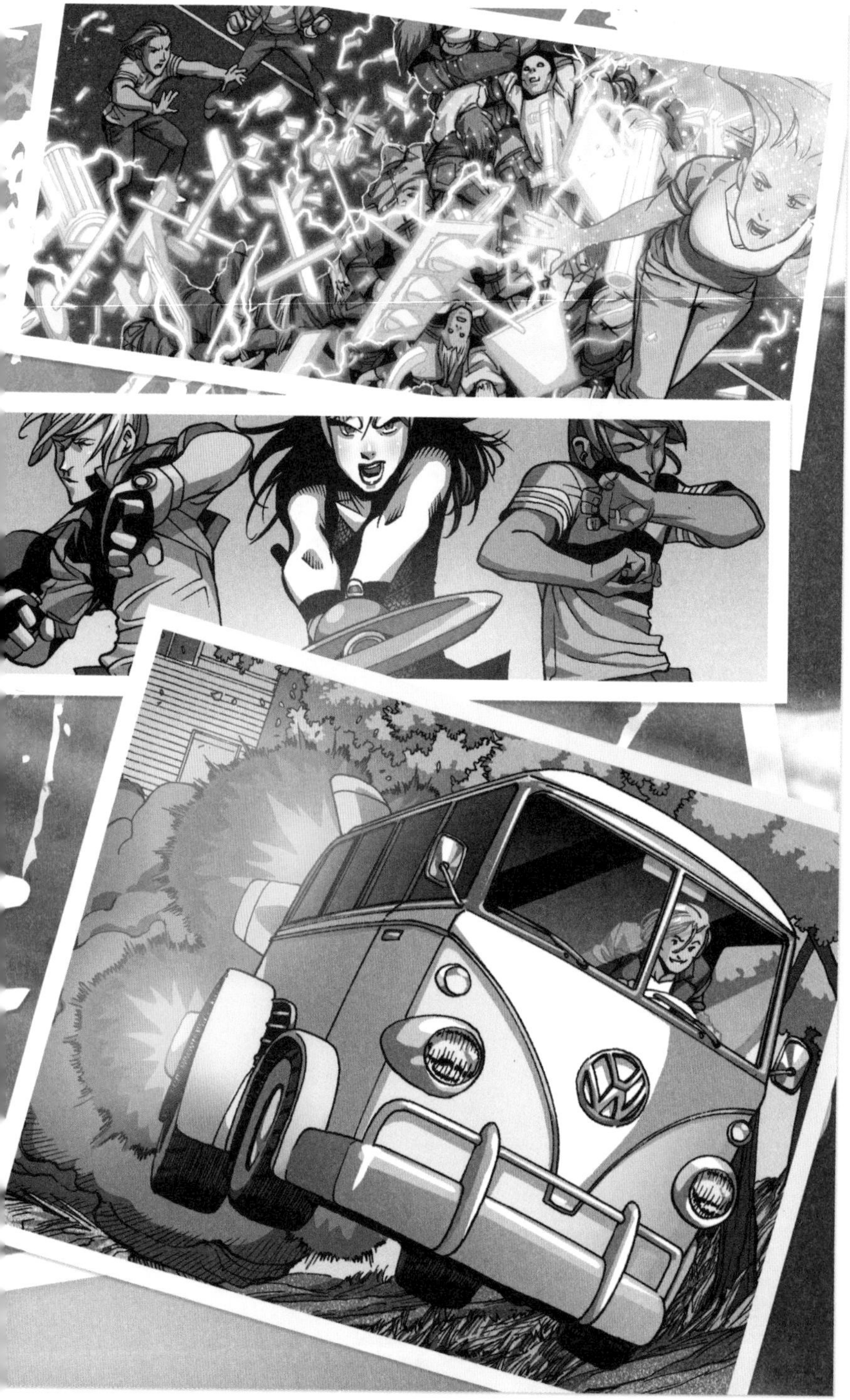

PREVIOUSLY

AT SOME POINT IN THEIR LIVES, ALL KIDS THINK THAT THEIR PARENTS ARE EVIL. FOR MOLLY HAYES AND HER FRIENDS, THIS IS ESPECIALLY TRUE. ONE NIGHT, MOLLY AND HER FRIENDS DISCOVERED THAT THEIR PARENTS WERE A GROUP OF SUPER-POWERED CRIME BOSSES WHO CALLED THEMSELVES "THE PRIDE." USING TECHNOLOGY AND RESOURCES STOLEN FROM THEIR PARENTS, THE TEENAGERS WERE ABLE TO STOP THE PRIDE AND BREAK THEIR CRIMINAL HOLD ON LOS ANGELES. BUT THEY'VE BEEN ON THE RUN EVER SINCE.

ATTACKED BY A CREW OF MAJESDANIAN SOLDIERS INTENT ON CAPTURING THE RUNAWAYS' KAROLINA DEAN—WHOM THEY HOLD RESPONSIBLE FOR THE DESTRUCTION OF THEIR HOME PLANET—THE RUNAWAYS FIGHT BACK AND DO EVERYTHING THEY CAN TO ESCAPE. BUT WHEN THEY REALIZE THAT THIS IS A FIGHT THEY WON'T BE ABLE TO WIN, THE SHAPESHIFTING XAVIN TAKES KAROLINA'S PLACE AND WILLINGLY AGREES TO GO WITH THE MAJESDANIANS, LEAVING HER FELLOW RUNAWAYS BEHIND.

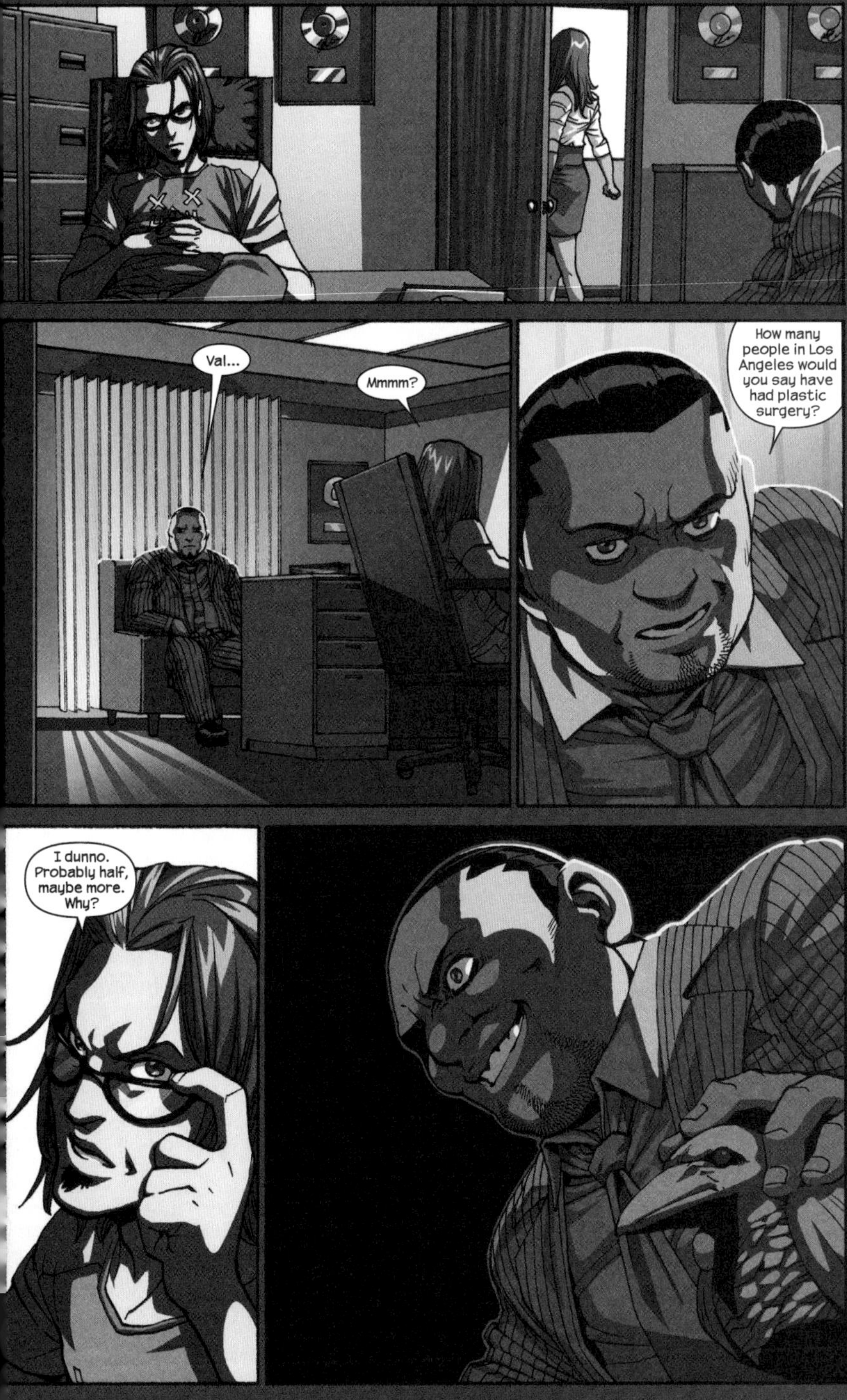
Val...
Mmmm?
How many people in Los Angeles would you say have had plastic surgery?
I dunno. Probably half, maybe more. Why?

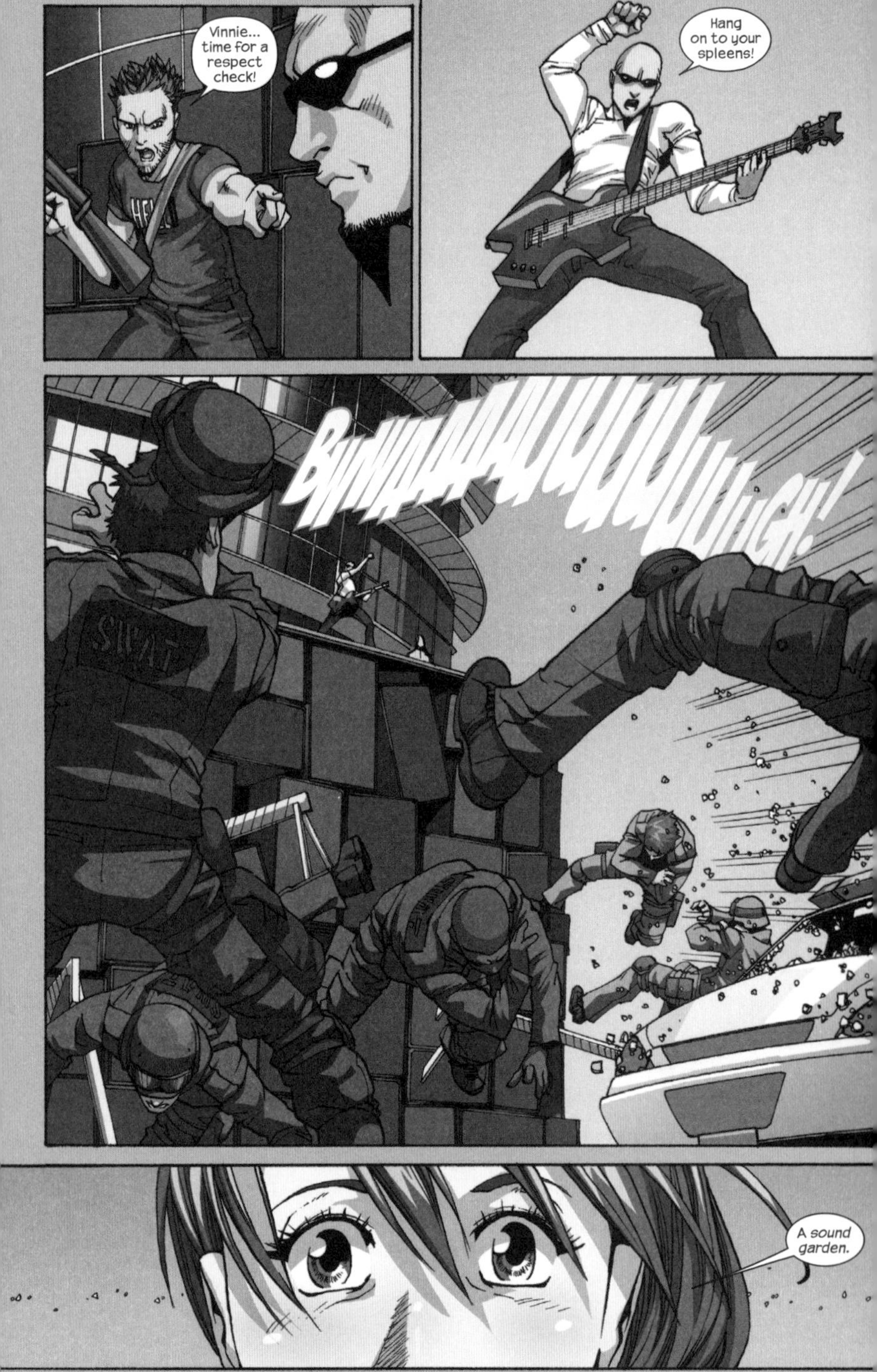
Vinnie... time for a respect check!
Hang on to your spleens!
BWHAAAAOUUUUUUUUGH!
A sound garden.

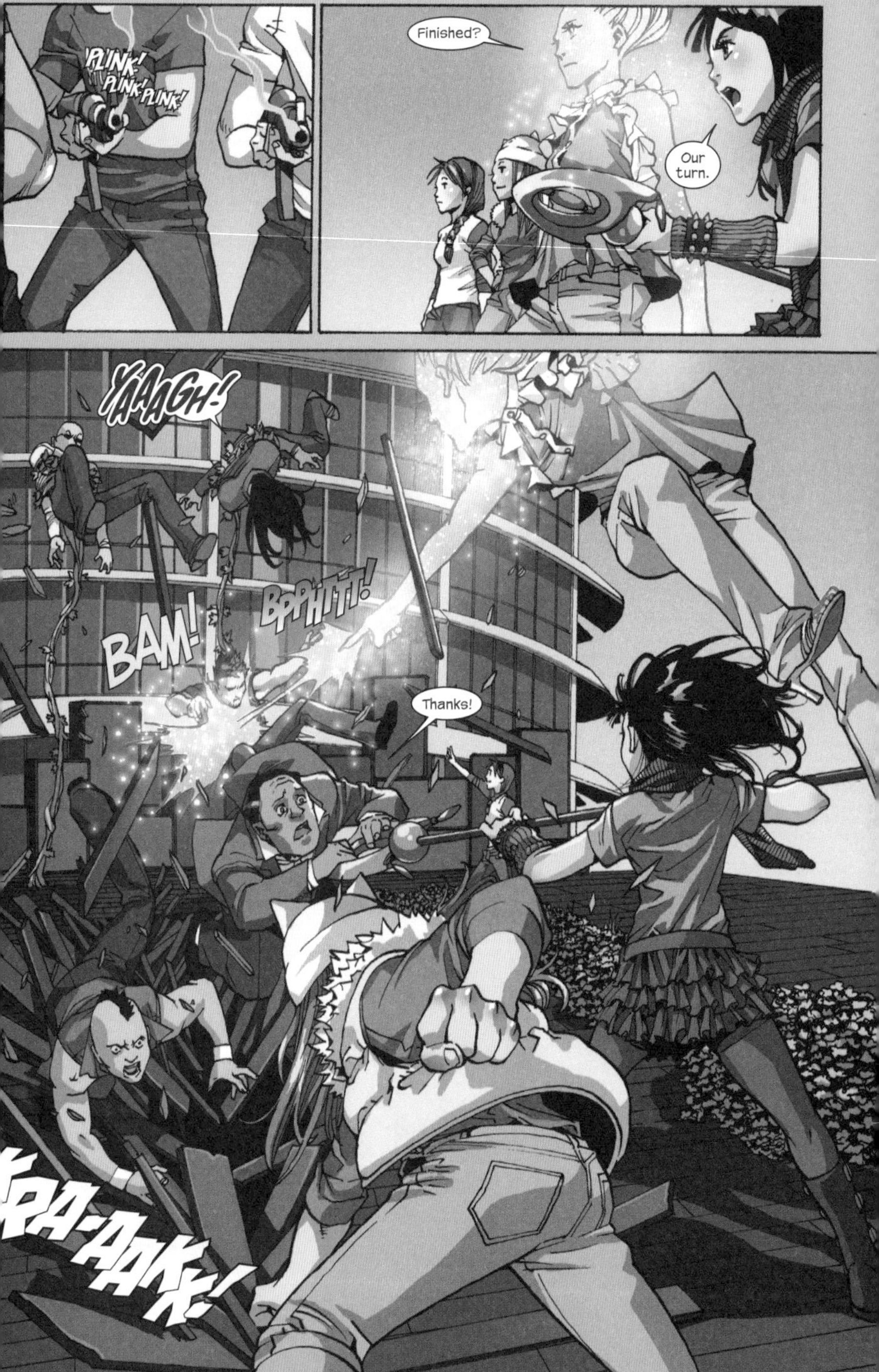

PLINK! PLINK! PLINK! PLINK!
Finished?
Our turn.
YAAAGH!
BPPHTTT!
BAM!
Thanks!
KRA-AAKK!

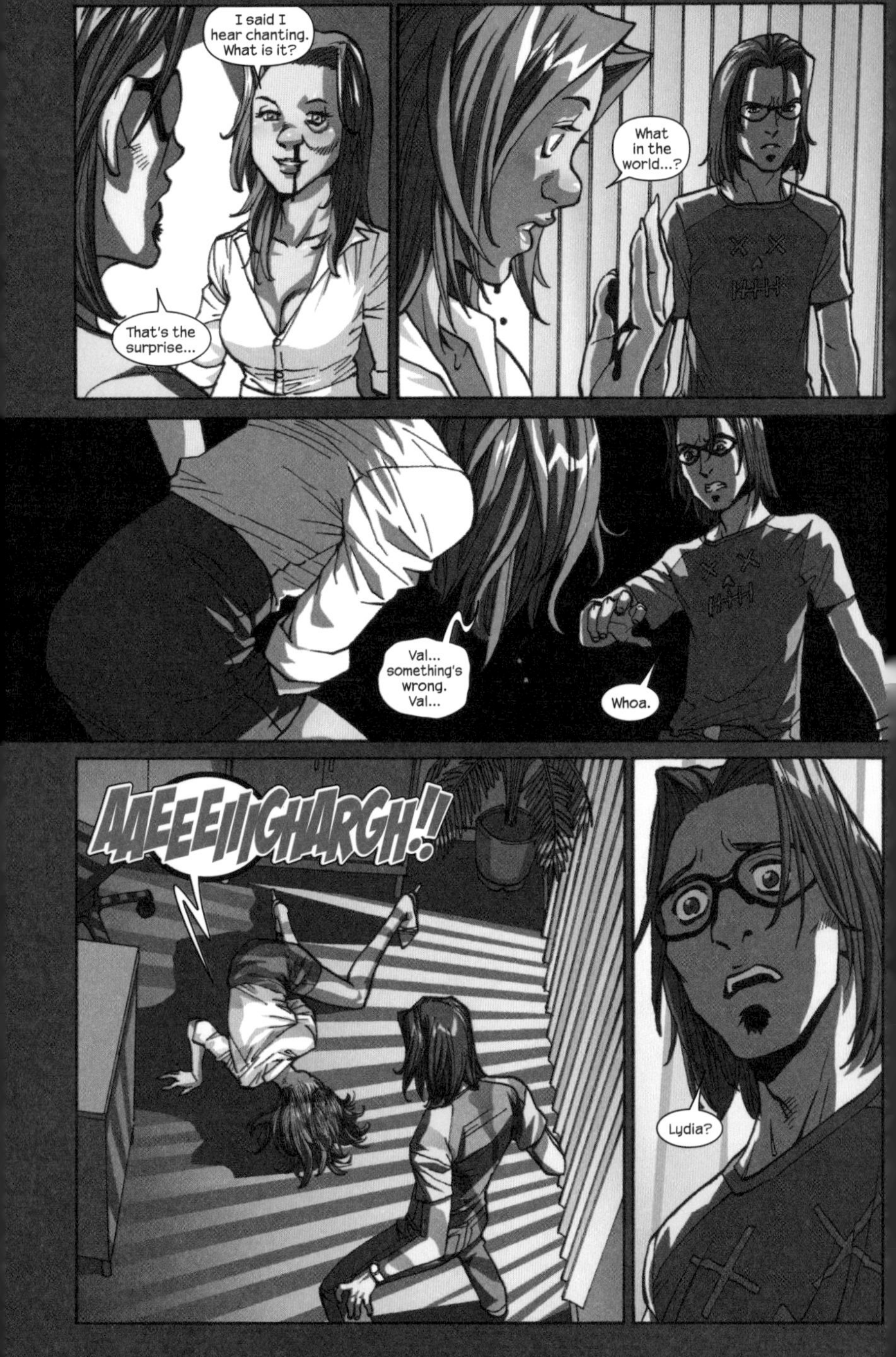
I said I hear chanting. What is it?
That's the surprise...
What in the world...?
Val... something's wrong. Val...
Whoa.
AAEEEIIIGHARGH!!
Lydia?

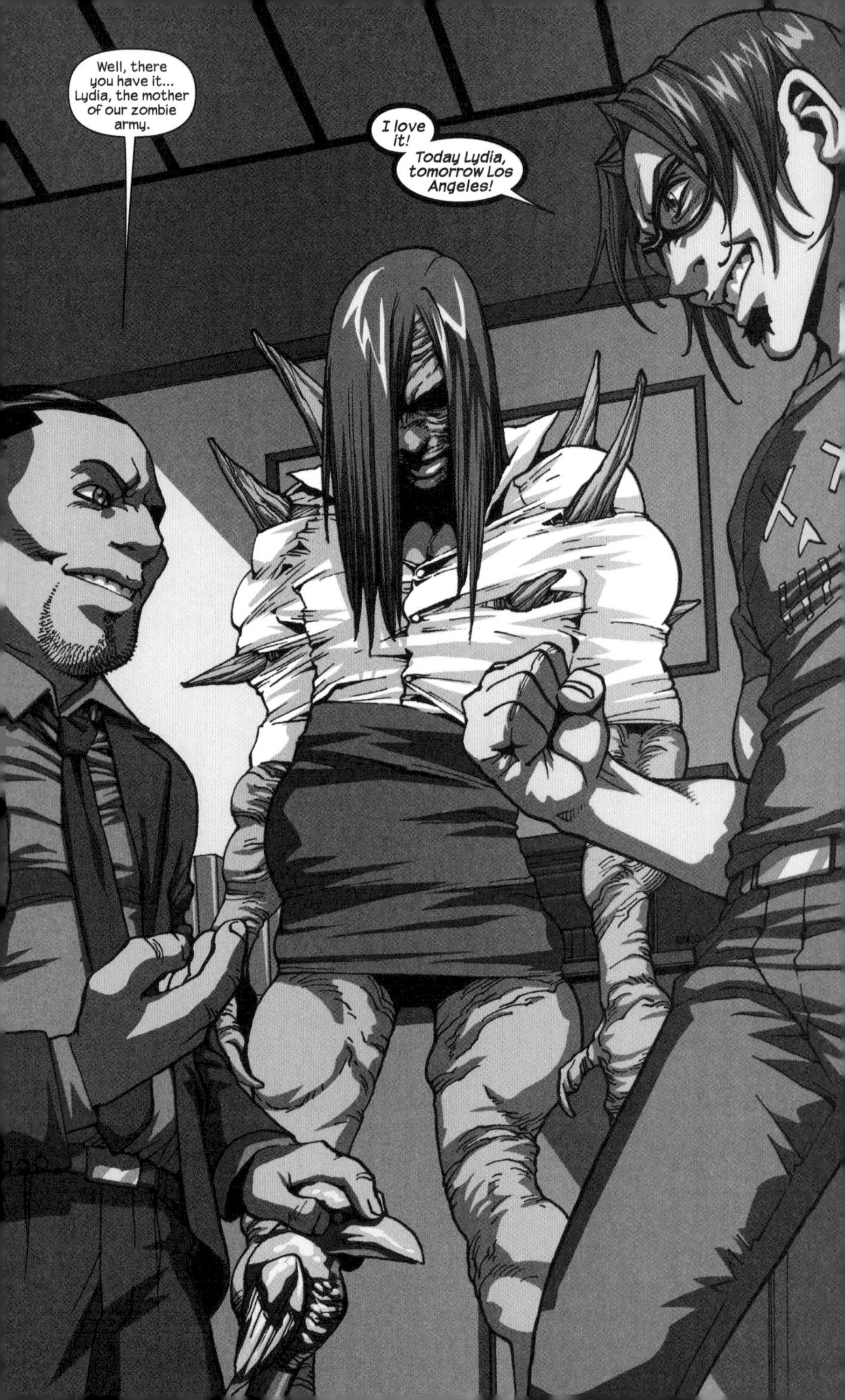
Well, there you have it... Lydia, the mother of our zombie army.
I love it!
Today Lydia, tomorrow Los Angeles!

8

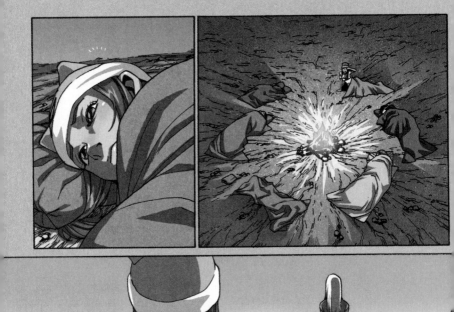

Mornin'.

Hey, K.

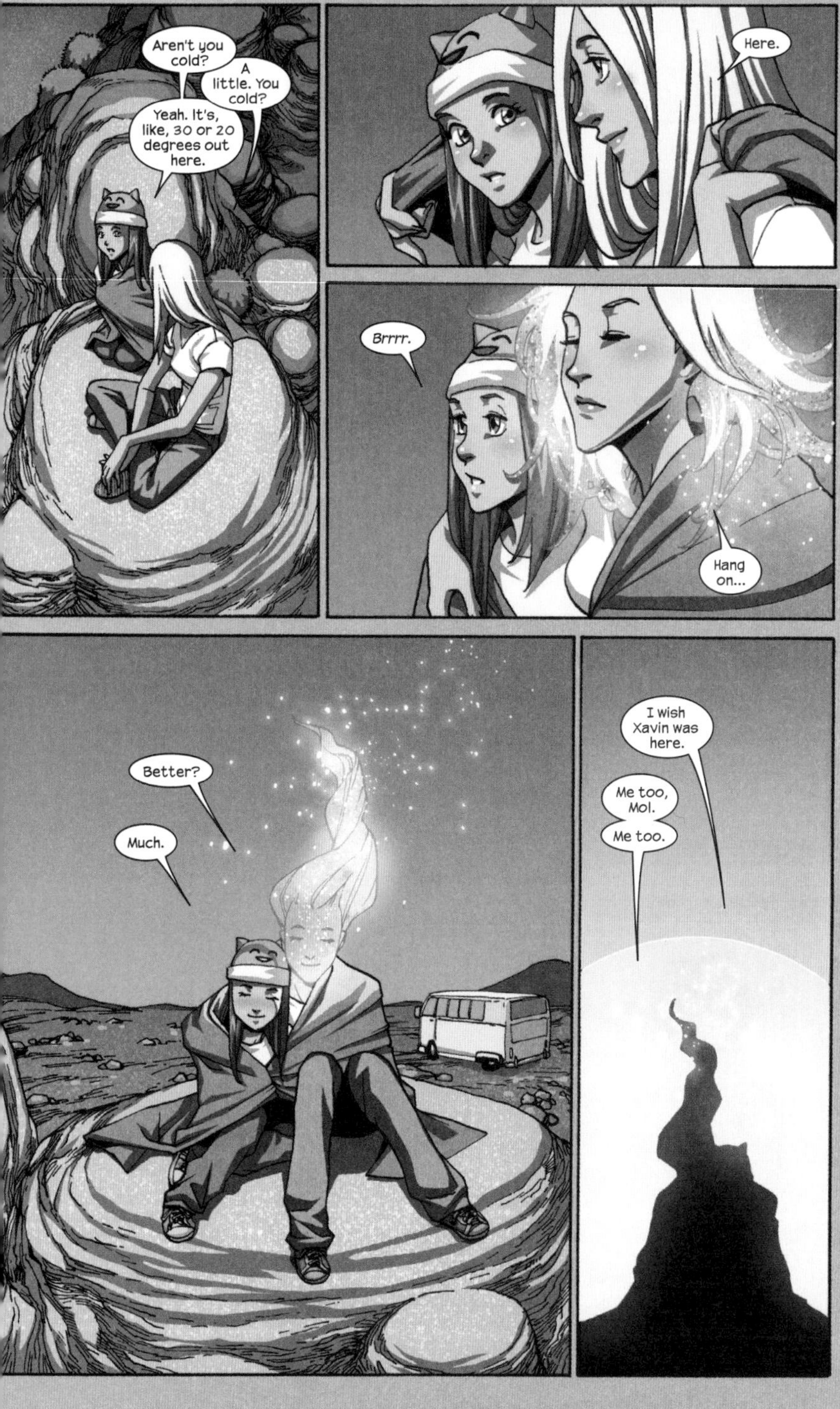

Aren't you cold?
A little. You cold?
Yeah. It's, like, 30 or 20 degrees out here.
Here.
Brrrr.
Hang on...
Better?
Much.
I wish Xavin was here.
Me too, Mol.
Me too.

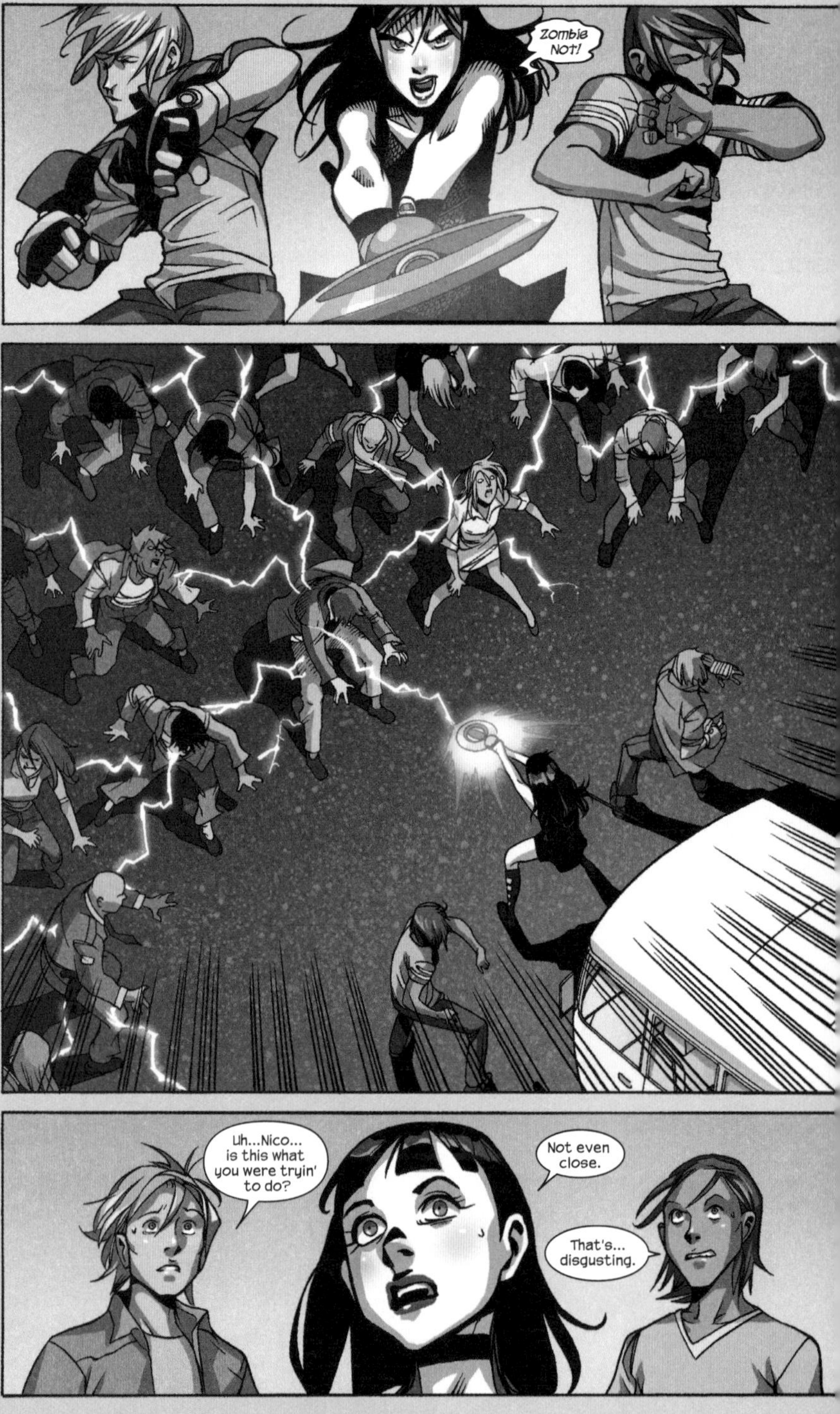
Zombie Not!
Uh...Nico... is this what you were tryin' to do?
Not even close.
That's... disgusting.

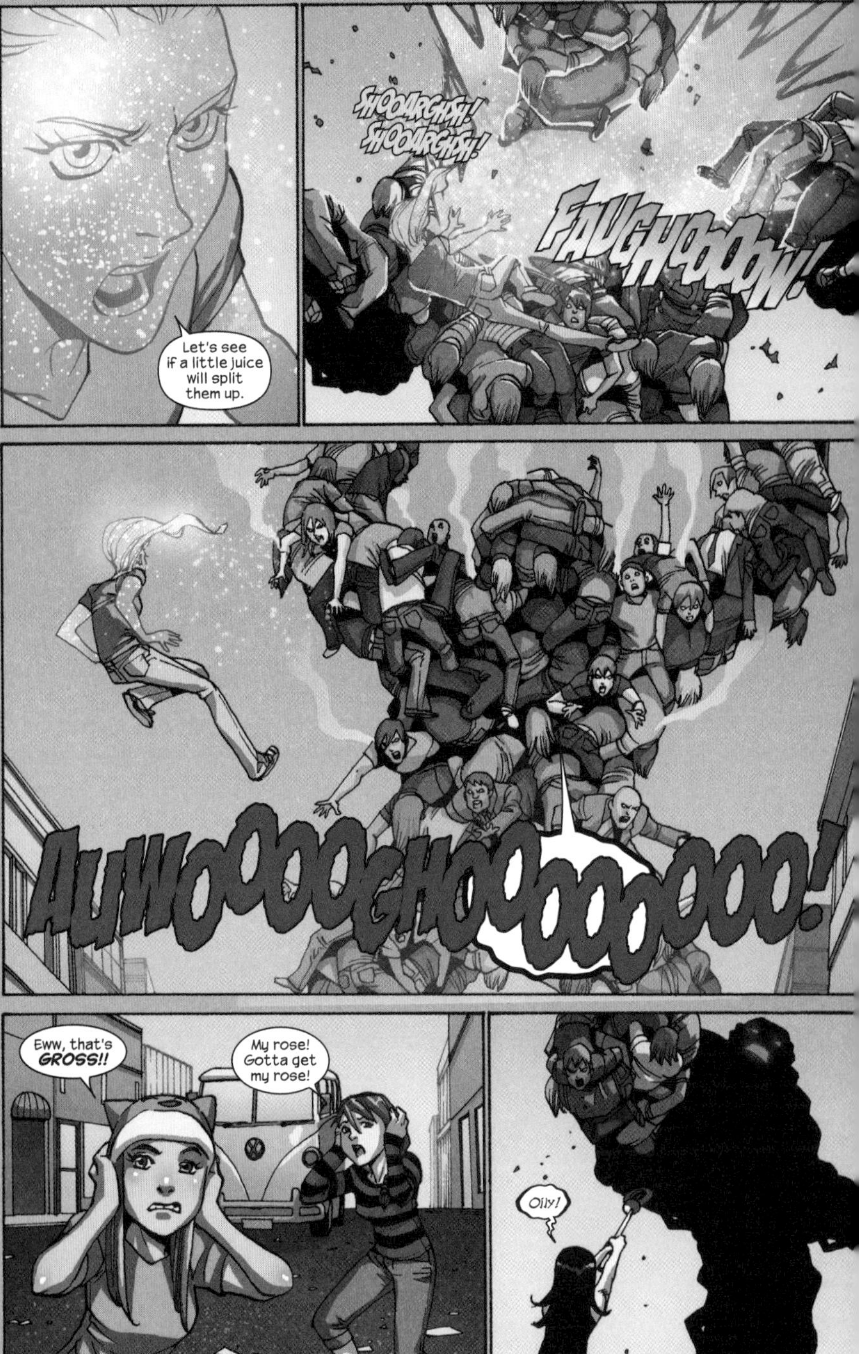
Let's see if a little juice will split them up.
SHOOARGHSH! SHOOARGHSH!
FAUGHOOOOW!
AUWOOOOGHOOOOOOOO!
Eww, that's **GROSS!!**
My rose! Gotta get my rose!
Olly!

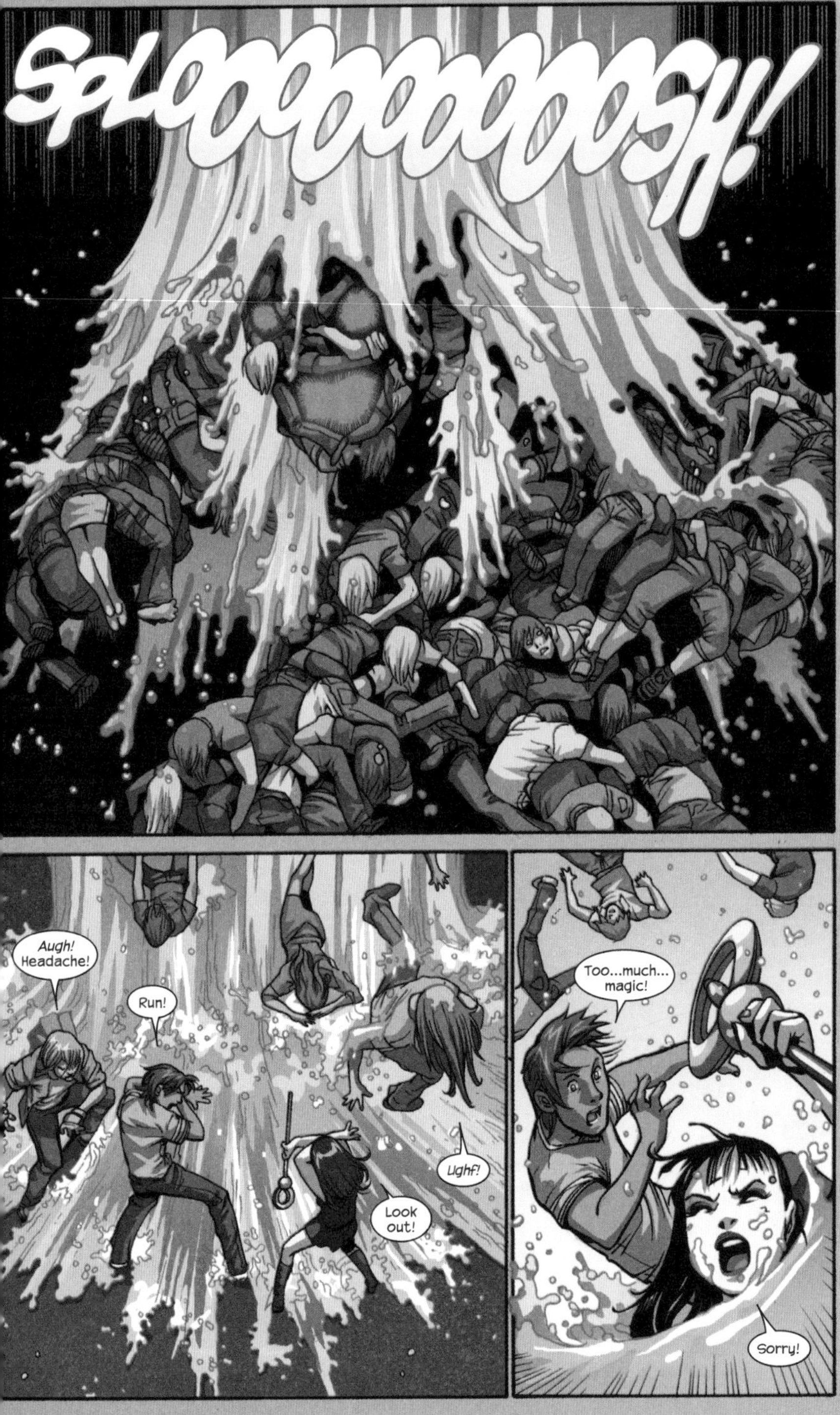
SPLOOOOOOOOOSH!
Augh! Headache!
Run!
Ughf!
Look out!
Too...much... magic!
Sorry!

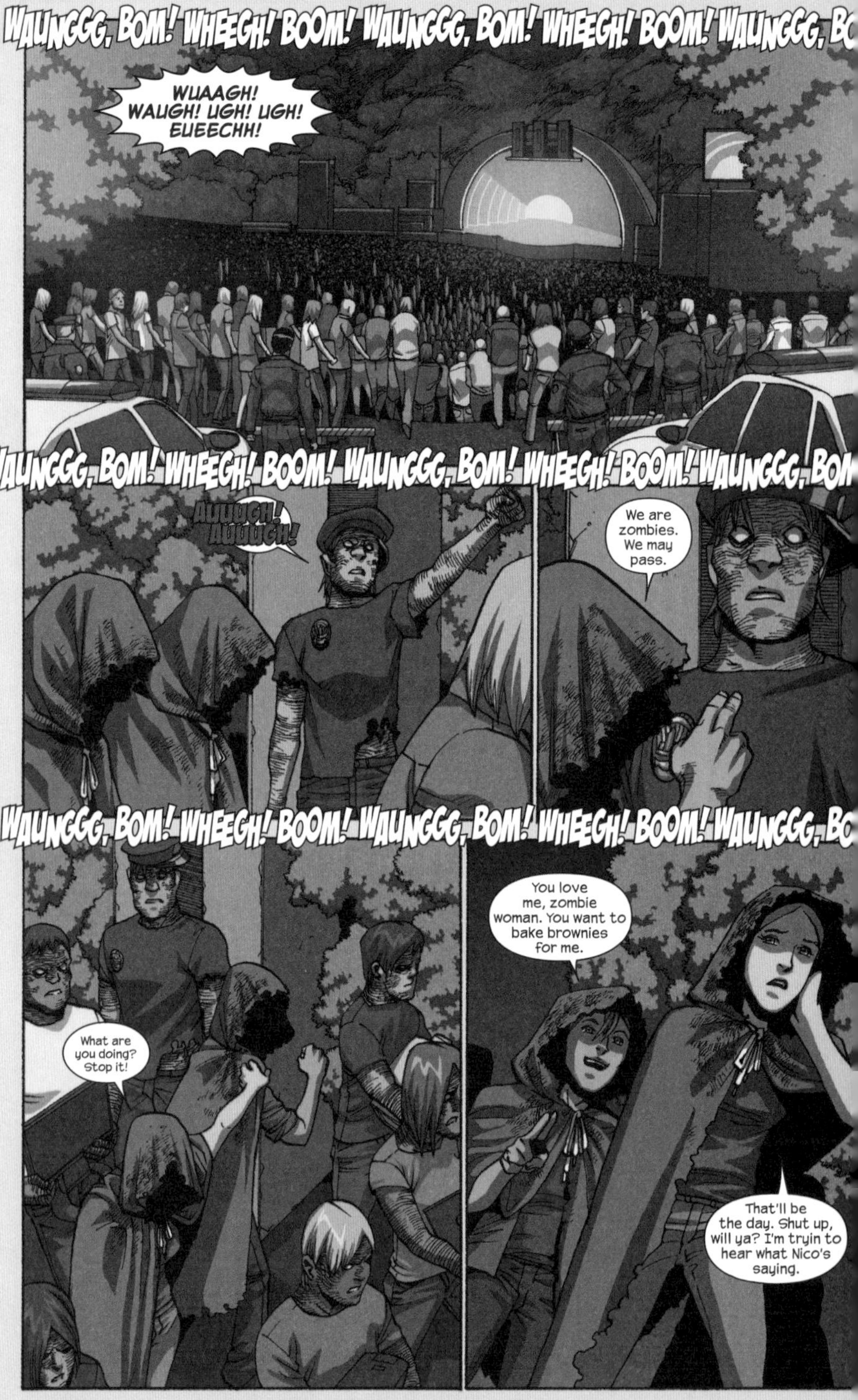
WAUNGGG, BOM! WHEEGH! BOOM! WAUNGGG, BOM! WHEEGH! BOOM! WAUNGGG, BO
WUAAGH! WAUGH! UGH! UGH! EUEECHH!
WAUNGGG, BOM! WHEEGH! BOOM! WAUNGGG, BOM! WHEEGH! BOOM! WAUNGGG, BOM
AUUUGH! AUUUGH!
We are zombies. We may pass.
WAUNGGG, BOM! WHEEGH! BOOM! WAUNGGG, BOM! WHEEGH! BOOM! WAUNGGG, BO
What are you doing? Stop it!
You love me, zombie woman. You want to bake brownies for me.
That'll be the day. Shut up, will ya? I'm tryin to hear what Nico's saying.

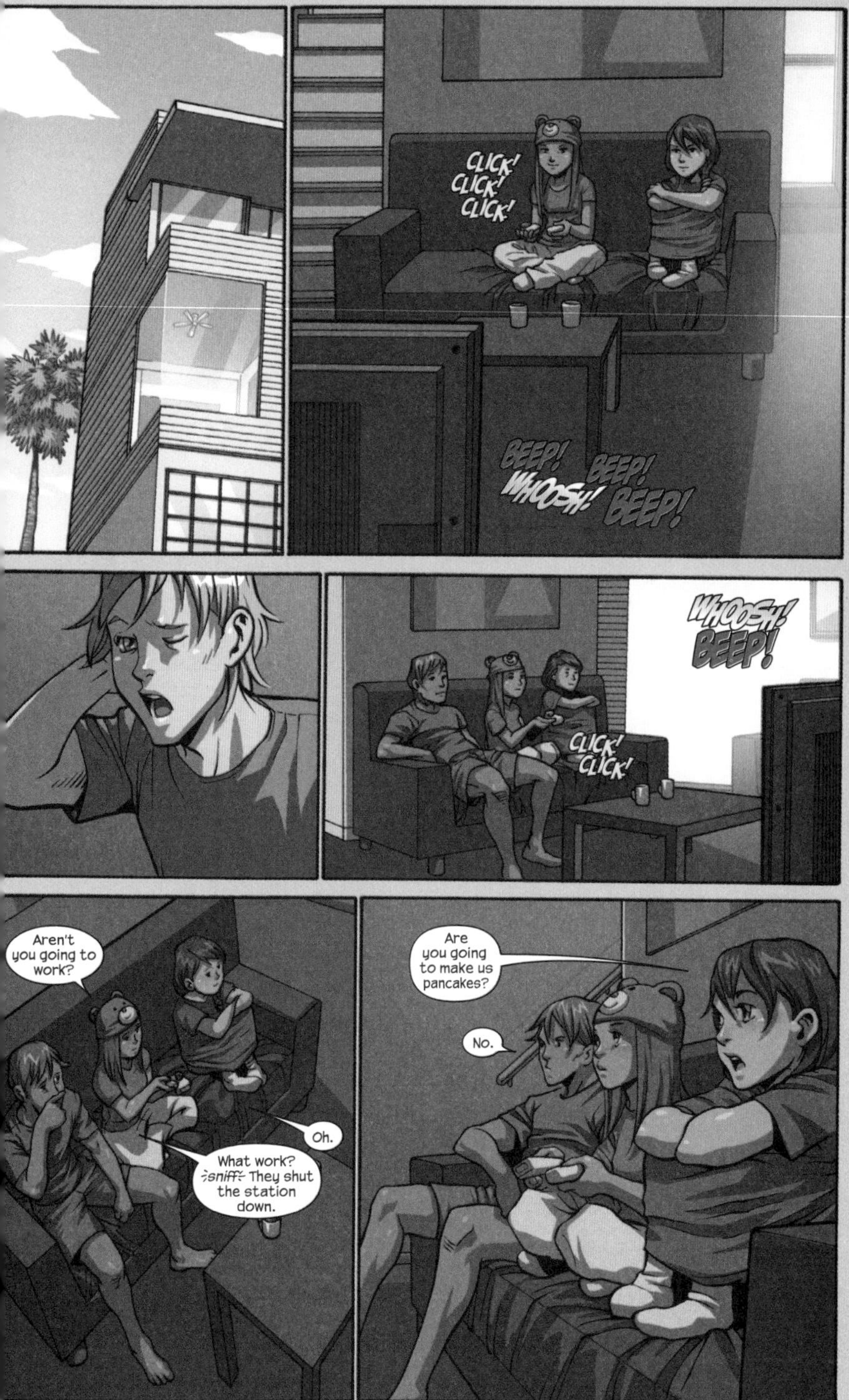
CLICK! CLICK! CLICK!
BEEP! WHOOSH! BEEP! BEEP!
WHOOSH! BEEP!
CLICK! CLICK!
Aren't you going to work?
Oh.
What work? =sniff= They shut the station down.
Are you going to make us pancakes?
No.

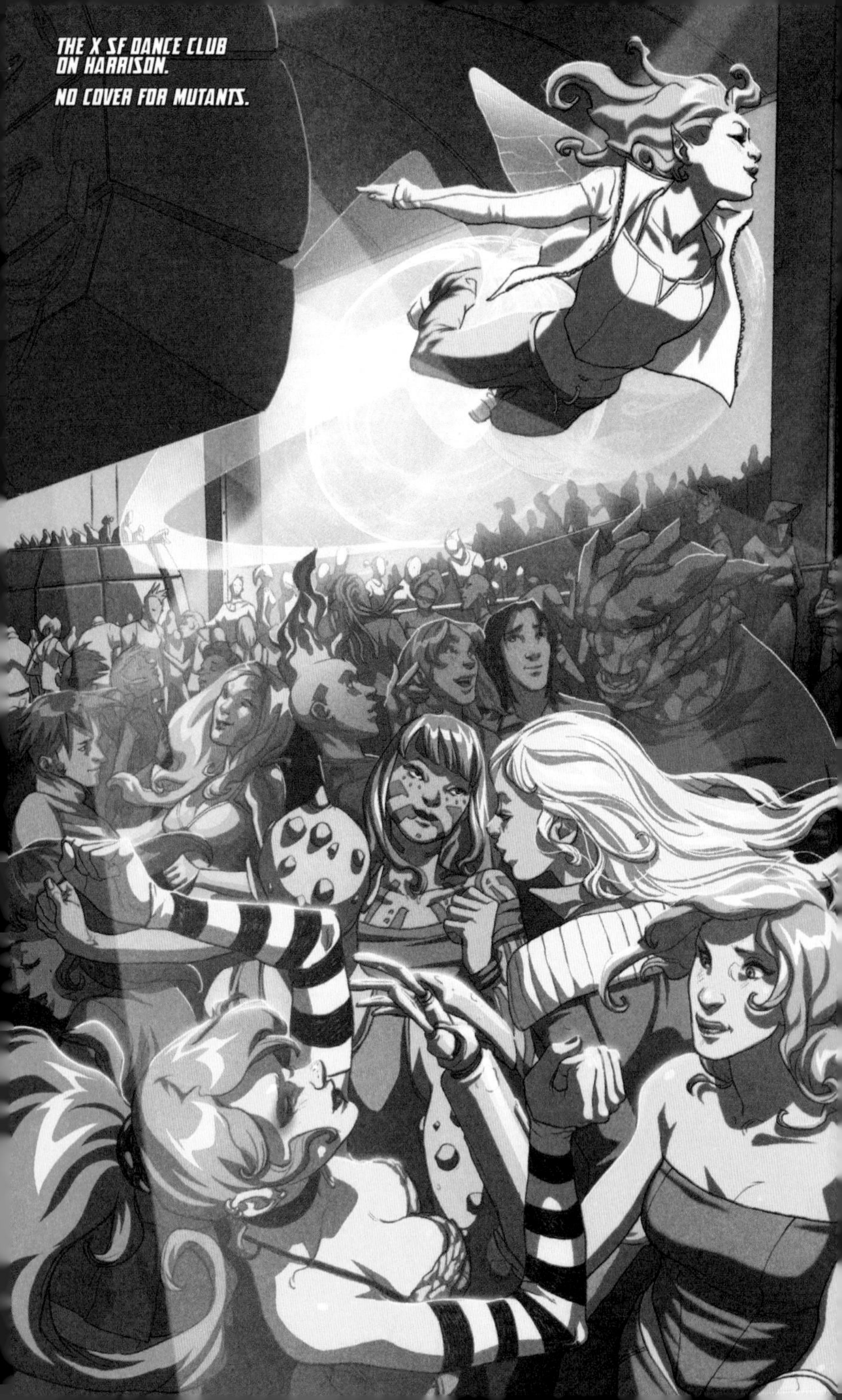
THE X SF DANCE CLUB ON HARRISON.
NO COVER FOR MUTANTS.

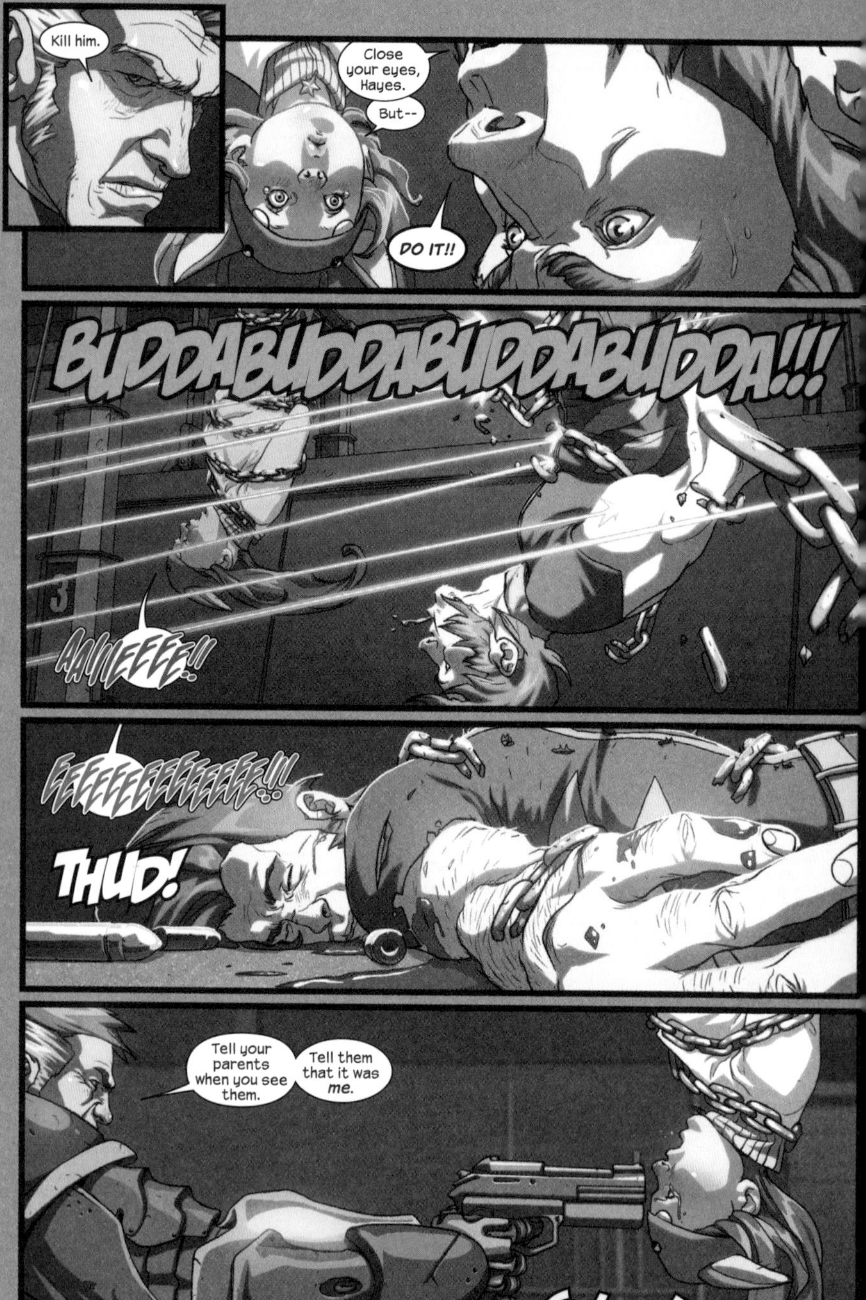
Kill him.
Close your eyes, Hayes.
But--
DO IT!!
BUDDABUDDABUDDABUDDA!!!
AAIIEEEE!!
EEEEEEEEEEEEE!!!
THUD!
Tell your parents when you see them.
Tell them that it was *me*.
SNIKT!!

Hear me, Sons of the Serpent!! With this staff we will lay waste to our foes! Finally ours will be the power unrivaled! And we will be the salvation of these United States of America! Lo! These many years has this great nation been systematically poisoned by the inferior genetics of foreigners! Mutants! Space men! Robot people! And worst of all--

WHHOOOOOOOOSH

Well, crap.

THE END.

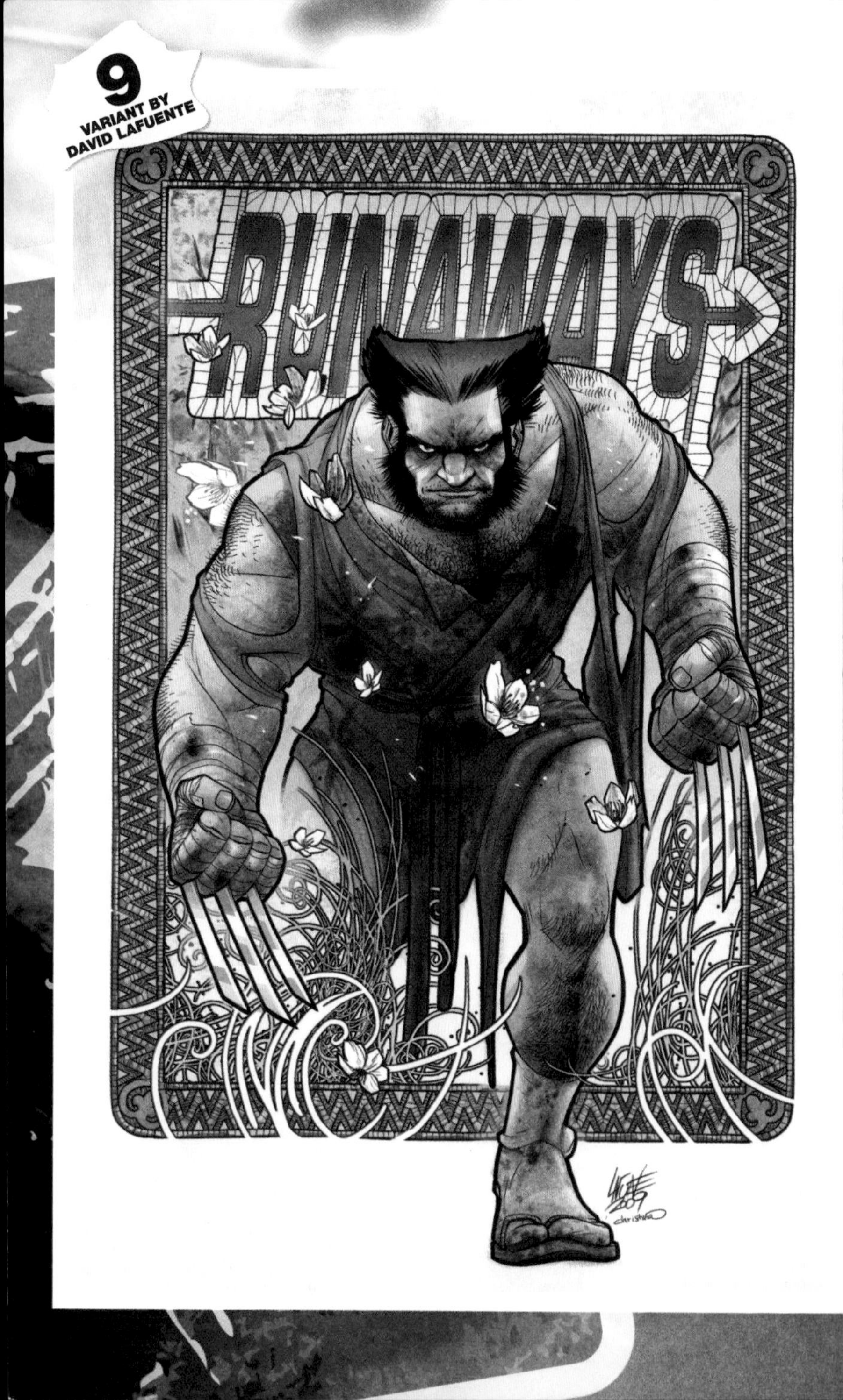

9
VARIANT BY
DAVID LAFUENTE
RUNAWAYS

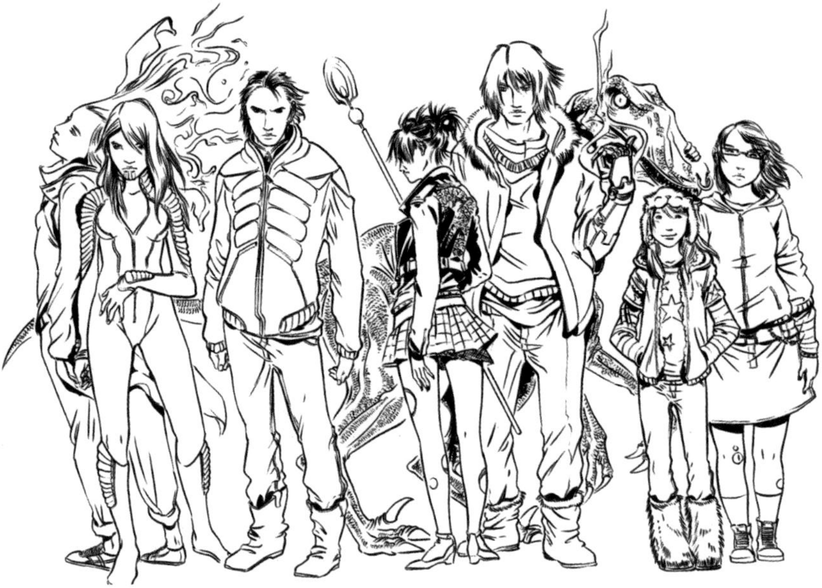

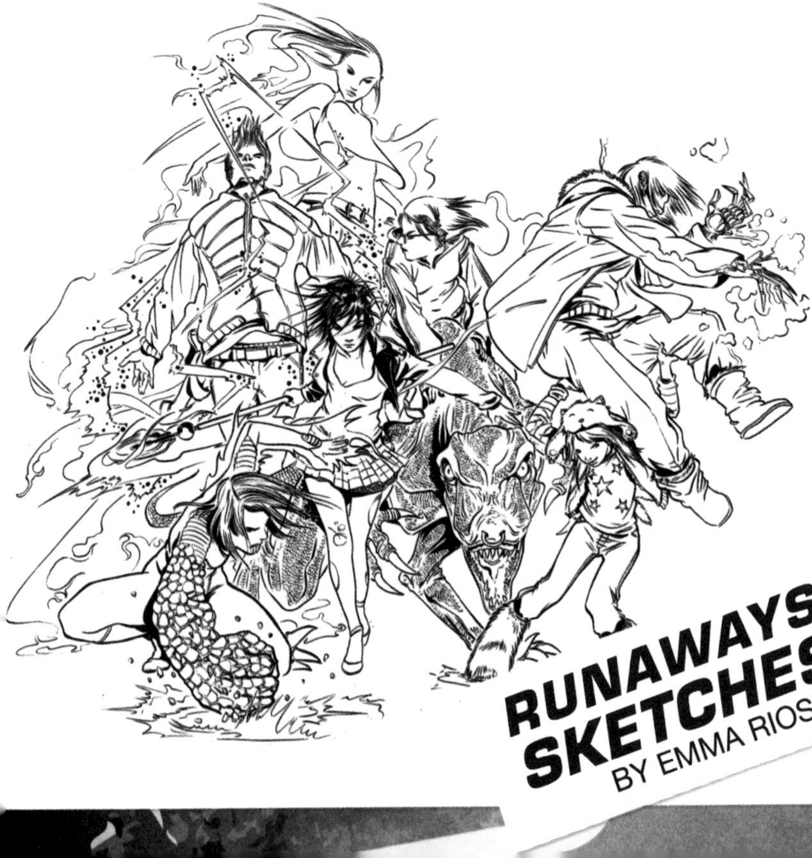

RUNAWAYS SKETCHES

BY EMMA RIOS

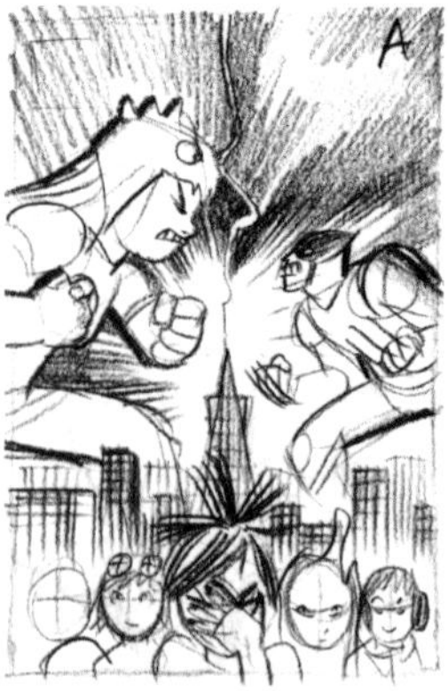
A

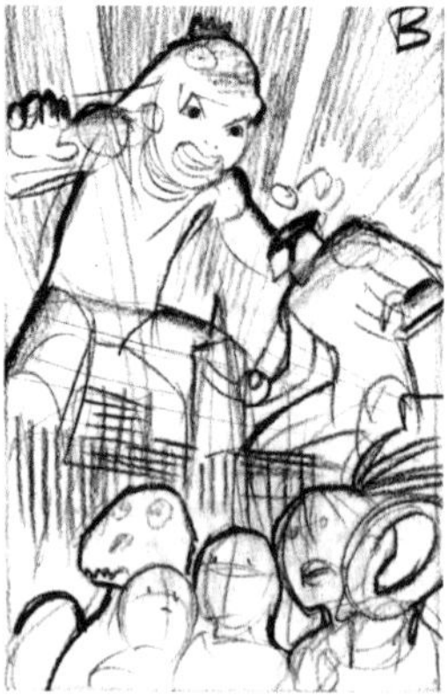
B

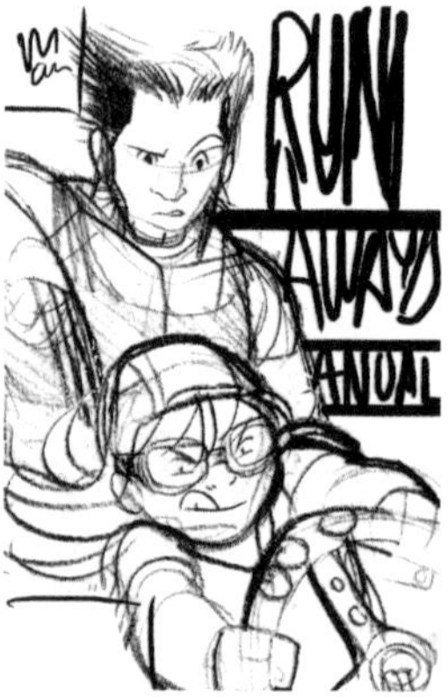

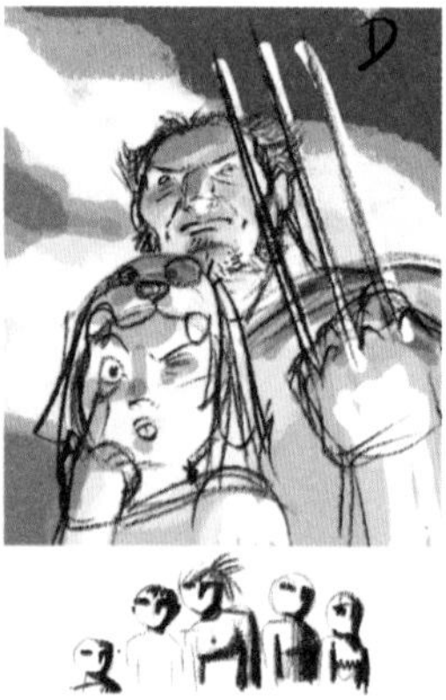
D

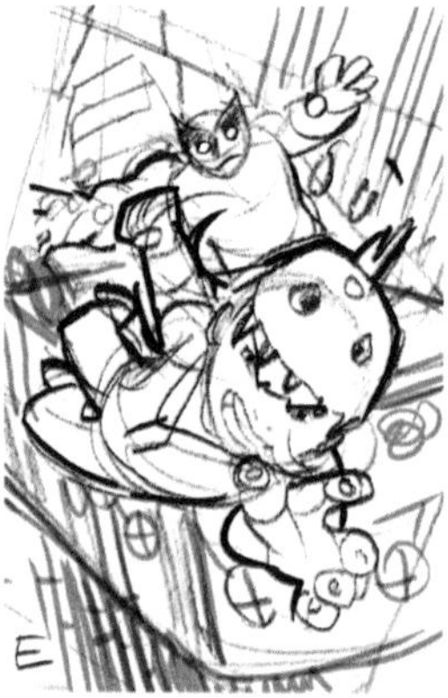
E

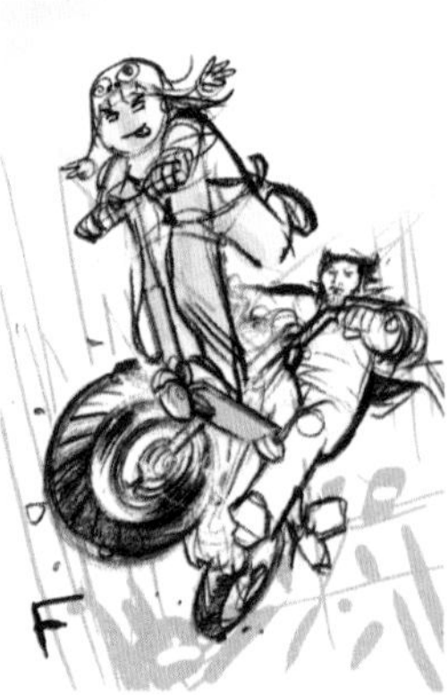
F

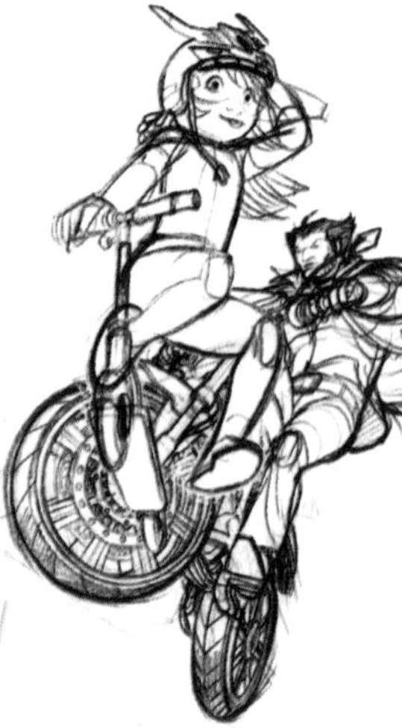

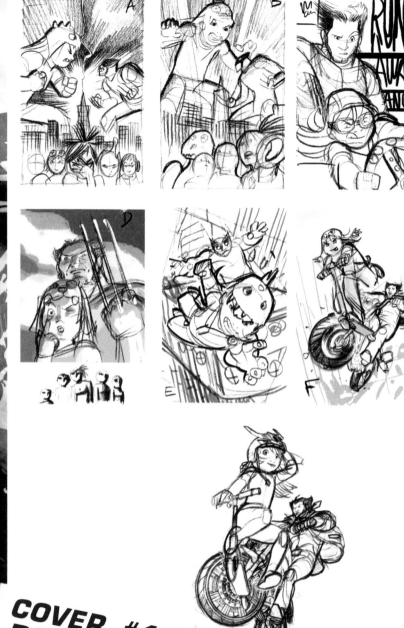

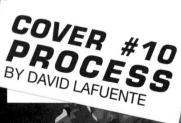

COVER #10 PROCESS
BY DAVID LAFUENTE

INKS

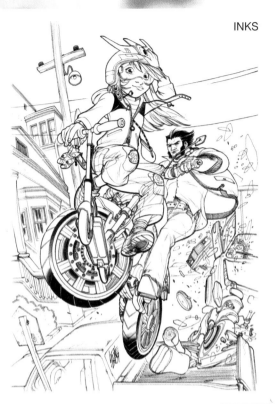

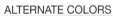

ALTERNATE COLORS

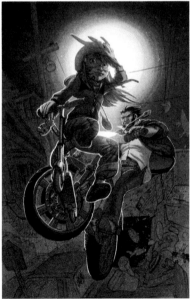

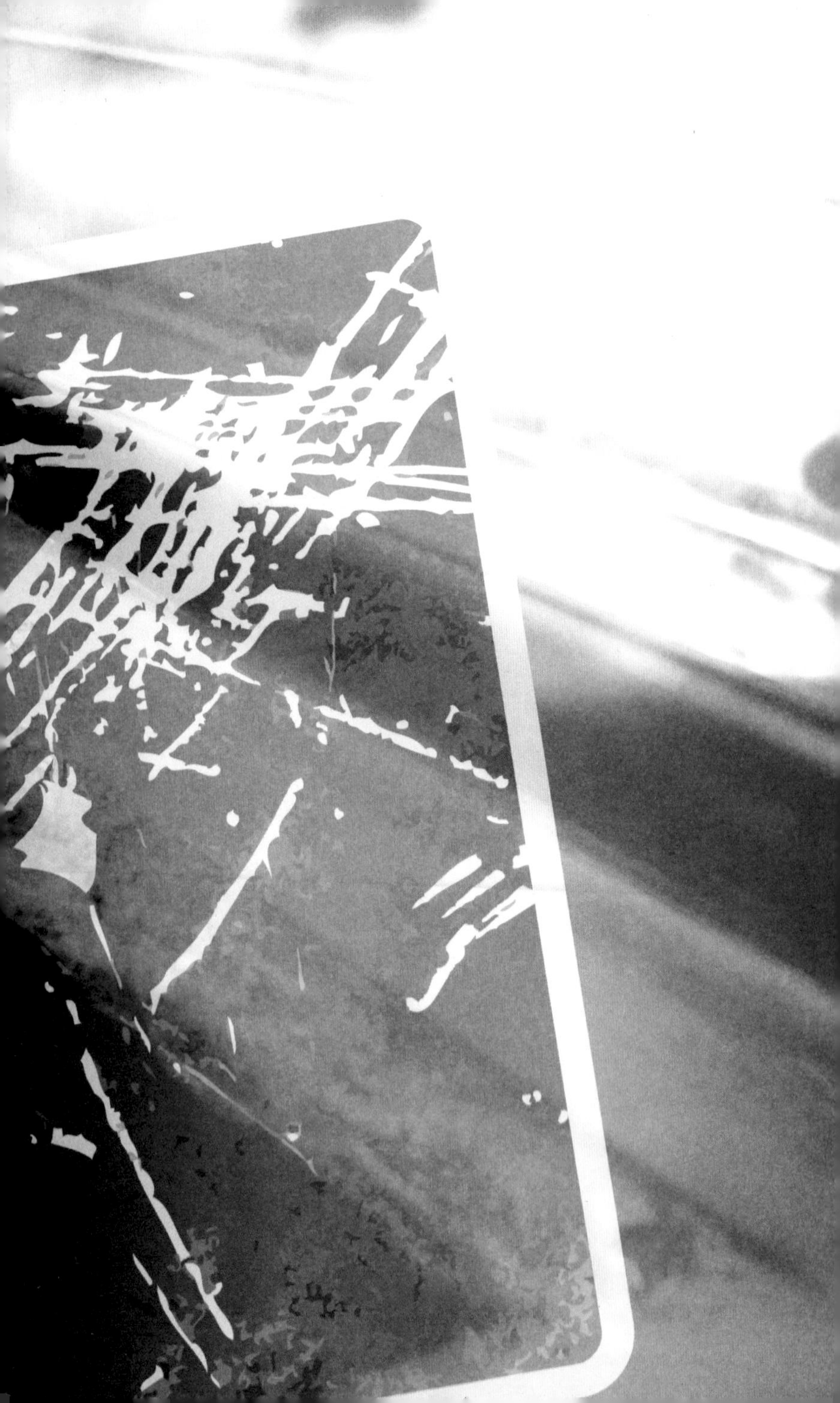